Spiritual Encounters

My Testimony

Velma Lyons Barr

Copyright © 2020 by Velma Lyons Barr
Spiritual Encounters: My Testimony
prayerbarr@hotmail.com

All rights reserved. In accordance with the U.S. Copyright Act of 1976, the scanning, uploading, and electronic sharing of any part of this book without the permission of the publisher is unlawful piracy and theft of the author's intellectual property. If you would like to use material from the book, prior written permission must be obtained by contacting the publisher at info@entegritypublishing.com.

Thank you for your support of the author's rights.

The views expressed in this work are solely those of the author and do not necessarily reflect the views of the publisher, and the publisher hereby disclaims any responsibility for them.

All scriptures are from the King James Version of the bible unless otherwise noted.

Entegrity Choice Publishing
PO Box 453
Powder Springs, GA 30127
info@entegritypublishing.com
www.entegritypublishing.com
770.727.6517

Printed in the United States of America

Library of Congress Cataloging-in-Publication Data
ISBN 978-1-7351739-6-2
Library of Congress Control Number: 2020911303

Dedication

In Loving memory of my parents — the late Willie Lyons and Rose J. Wilson. I think about you every day, and I cherish the memories that we shared. I love you forever. Rest in peace.

"We are confident, yes well pleased, rather to be absent from the body and to be present with the Lord."
2 Corinthians 5:8 NKJV

Acknowledgements

I thank Our Lord and Savior, Jesus Christ. To Him I give all the Glory, Honor and Praise for the publishing of this book.

"And He showed me a pure river of water of life, clear as crystal, proceeding from the throne of God and of the Lamb."
Revelation 22:1

"Now unto Him that is able to do exceedingly abundantly above all that we ask or think, according to the power that worketh in us, unto Him be glory in the church by Christ Jesus throughout all ages, world without end."
Ephesians 3:20-21

To my husband, Kevin, I am truly grateful for your prayers, love, support, and words of encouragement. There were times that I knew you were tired, yet you never told me no. Instead, you gave me your heart. Whatever I needed, you made sure I had. Even days when you weren't feeling your

Acknowledgements

best, you came to my rescue. I'm forever grateful and will always cherish our union together. I love you, forever.

To my children Ebony, Natadra, and Kendrick — I am so proud of you all. We've been through some tough times, and God brought us through. I'm forever grateful. Thank you for your love, prayers, and support. I love you, dearly.

To my wonderful grandchildren — Janiya, Jovan Jr., Zariya, and Lennox — you bring me so much joy, and I thank God for you all. I love you, dearly.

To my sister, Ann, and her husband, Jeff: I cannot thank you enough for praying for me. Thank you for your encouraging words, patience, support and love. I'm forever grateful. I love you!

To my sister, Sally, and her husband, Andre: thank you for all the encouraging words, prayers, support, and your never-ending love. You always said to start somewhere, and I did. I love you, and I'm forever grateful.

To my sister, Debra, and her husband, Terry: I love you and appreciate the hot seat that Kevin and I always find ourselves in. We really enjoy ourselves, and for that we are forever grateful for your love, wisdom, prayers, and support.

Acknowledgements

To my awesome sons-in-law and daughter-in-law — Jovan, Courtland, and Briana — I thank God for bringing you all into our lives. We are forever grateful and love you all

To my family whom I love dearly, I thank God for each of you; even those who have passed on from this life. Words cannot express my love for you. Family, I love you.

Special thanks to Roxie Hairston and Entegrity Choice Publishing for making this book happen. God bless you all.

Special thanks to Mrs. Kristy Bank Jones. I truly appreciate the push; it was worth it all. I love you all.

I will be forever grateful for Minister Shirley Underwood. I truly thank God for this praying woman of God. I am thankful for our friendship; I love you.

I am so blessed to have Evangelist Annette Williams in my life. Thank you for your encouraging words, your wisdom, and your prayers. I love you dearly.

I thank God for my church family, Fairview Missionary Baptist Church - I love you all.

Contents

Dedication 3

Acknowledgements 5

Introduction 11

Chapter One
    My Childhood 15

Chapter Two
    Angel Experience.................... 19

Chapter Three
    The Preacher and The Deacon 23

Chapter Four
    Church Of God In Christ (COGIC) 27

Chapter Five
    Newborn Babe in Christ 31

Chapter Six
    Water 35

Chapter Seven
    Bedroom Visitation 39

Contents

Chapter Eight
 The Couch 43

Chapter Nine
 The Floor 47

Chapter Ten
 Hell 51

Chapter Eleven
 Heaven 57

Chapter Twelve
 Joy 61

Chapter Thirteen
 Love 65

Introduction

I've heard over and over, "Write the vision, and make it plain." After being silent for so many years, I knew it was time to open up and tell my story.

I really believe my story will encourage and inspire others to tell their stories. I must be honest: fear had gripped my heart, and I was wrestling within myself whether to come forward or not. I can truly say as I put this on paper, I'm so glad I did.

I had to step out of my comfort zone and begin to move by faith. Facing the unknown can be fearful at times, and even challenging.

"For God hath not given us the spirit of fear; but of power, and of love, and of a sound mind."
2 Timothy 1:7

Knowing that God is with me, and I can do all things through Christ who strengthen me, I pressed forward to tell my story. All glory and honor go to

Introduction

my Lord and Savior, Jesus Christ.

Here is what I experienced: my spirit left my body, and I was just thrilled and amazed. I have never experienced anything like this before. This is beyond the natural realm; it's the spiritual realm.

Hell is a very dark, foul, horrible place where there is screaming, yelling, and crying. This is what I saw and heard. Suddenly, the hand of God pulled me out of Hell and allowed me to see Heaven.

Heaven is an exquisite place. Once you are there, you don't want to leave because it's so peaceful. I wanted to stay, but couldn't because He said that it wasn't my time. Oh, how I long to stay there. It was so peaceful to the point that nothing else mattered. This peace can only be given by the Lord Himself because it came from Him.

Months later, I had another visitation where I was floating in a river of crystal water so bright and sparkly, and moving so graceful. The water covered me up to my neck. I had no fear as I floated in the water, only peace. Then, suddenly, a very large hand picked me up out of the water, and He carried me in His hand, letting me know that everything was alright.

I want everyone to know that there is life after

you take your last breath. This is the beginning of living forever in Heaven or in Hell. I pray that if you have not accepted Jesus into your heart, do it today. Choose ye this day whom you will serve.

1

My Childhood

*"Train up a child in the way he should go:
and when he is old, he will not depart from it."
Proverbs 22:6*

I appreciate the foundation my mom gave to me and my sisters. My sisters and I were raised in a Baptist church where we all sang in the choir, attended vacation Bible school, went to Sunday school, and participated in many church activities.

Mom made sure we knew about the Lord. I didn't understand it then, but now I do. Mom prayed all the time and sang songs of praise. Mom wanted the best for my sisters and me. She worked hard to provide for us. She never once gave up. Mom expressed her love in many ways. She loved her girls, and we loved her too. We thank God for our mom, as well as our dad. Mom taught us this scripture at an early age:

*"Children obey your parents in the Lord, for this
is right. Honor your father and mother,
which is the first commandment with promise:
that it may be well with you and
you may live long on the earth."
Ephesians 6:1-3 NKJV*

My Childhood

Mom kept us well-groomed and dressed us in beautiful dresses and ruffled socks. Our home was always clean. We never once had a dirty house. Mom taught us, at an early age, how to keep a clean home. Today, I can still say that's how we live.

When I was about seven years old, my mom divorced my dad because he had some issues that he had been dealing with for several years. This caused the family to go separate ways. My sister and I went with my mom. My dad never gave up on us because of his love for us, and he was very protective of us.

My dad had a heart of gold. His passions were yardwork and cooking. Being separated was sad at times, but it was for the best. Dad gave up that bad habit he had because his health was decreasing. Today, Dad is resting in peace, and so is Mom. Sleep on in the presence of the Lord. I love you.

2
Angel Experience

One day, I was leaving the hair salon after getting my hair washed and pressed. On this particular day, as I was walking along the path, I heard a voice say, "Look up." I did just that. Oh my! What fearsome sight! There was an angel right above me in the sky. I really didn't know what to expect from the angel. My heart began to beat at a fast. pace. I panicked and took off running. The angel kept floating above me so peacefully in the sky.

The angel's face was like the face of a person but it had a glow on it. The angel had on a long, white gown with the colors purple, scarlet, and gold. They were the most beautiful colors I had ever seen. The angel had a gold horn in its mouth. No sound was coming out of the horn.

The angel just kept floating in the sky and followed me as I was running. The angel followed me all the way home. I ran into the house with excitement in my voice, yelling, "Mommy! There's an angel in the sky, and it followed me home!" My mom was bewildered.

3

The Preacher and The Deacon

After I saw the angel, there was a knock at the door. It was our pastor and one of the deacons from the church. The pastor and deacon would walk and visit church members. Our church was about fifteen minutes away in walking distance from our house.

Mom began to tell the pastor and the deacon about my experience with the angel. She told them that I saw an angel in the sky, and it followed me home. The pastor and the deacon had excitement on their faces. It made me feel good to know that they believed me. The pastor said to Mom, "If she said she saw an angel, let's not doubt it, Rose. It can happen. It's okay."

After talking, we headed to the backyard, looked up, and the angel was gone. I will never forget that experience.

"For He shall give his Angels charge over thee, to keep thee in all thy ways." Psalm 91:11

4

Church of God in Christ (COGIC)

Growing up, I had been in a Baptist Church as long as I could remember. After I graduated from school and moved to Florida, a few years later, I began to attend a church across the street from the house. What a surprise it was. It was a Church Of God In Christ church. I never had seen anything like this.

My children and I started attending the church, and what an awakening it was! We saw dancing and we heard this strange language some were speaking. The man on the organ was playing with a face full of joy.

I began to learn about Jesus and the devil. The tall man in the pulpit was wearing a long robe. He had an accent, and I learned that he was Jamaican. I thank the Lord for the bishop at that church. My husband and my children really loved him. Bishop would be preaching about holiness or Hell, Jesus or the devil. He preached the Word of God. He would say, "Get all you can, and can all you get."

I never heard the Bible so plainly as I did there. I heard that the devil is the father of lies. He comes to steal, kill, and destroy. Jesus came to give life, and to give it more abundantly.

"The thief cometh not, but for to steal and to kill, and to destroy. I am come that they might have life, and that they might have it more abundantly."
John 10:10

One day, as Bishop was preaching, something happened inside of me. I realized that he was talking about a real devil. He really had my attention. I wanted more of what I was hearing. The devil is evil, but God is love. I heard that God loves me unconditionally. He talked about Heaven and Hell. I was a Christian, but I didn't have a relationship with the Lord yet.

5
Newborn Babe in Christ

Being a newborn babe in Christ, I began to seek the Lord for myself. I heard the bishop say over and over, "Seek Him with your whole heart."

He would often quote Matthew 6:33 – "But seek ye first the kingdom of God and his righteousness, and all these things shall be added unto you."

Bishop would say, "Love God with all your heart, mind, and soul."

I began to pray like never before. I prayed for my mom, dad, sisters, family, and everyone who came to my mind. I didn't want anyone to die and go to Hell. I prayed for everyone to get a real relationship with the Lord. I had confidence, knowing that if I would seek Him, I would find Him.

As I continued to grow in my Christian walk, I came to know some ladies in the church called Missionaries. These were some praying women of God with power. Yes, power! They were anointed by the power of God. I was told to get on the altar and tarry, and that's exactly what I did. I got on the altar over and over.

I began to study my Bible, and the Holy Spirit taught me. When I first started reading, I didn't understand anything. So, I called my sister, and she said, "Keep reading, and God will give you understanding."

I did just as I was told, and one day I could understand everything that I was reading. Praise God!

The Holy Spirit gave me wisdom and understanding. As a newborn babe, I heard so much. That's why I had to go after Him and seek Him with my whole heart. "In His presence is fullness of joy." As I continued to seek Him, these scriptures were a blessing to me.

> *"For he who comes to God must believe that He is, and that He is rewarder of those who diligently seek Him."*
> *Hebrews 11:6b*

> *"So I say to you, ask, and it will be given to you; seek, and you will find; knock, and it will be opened to you. For everyone who asks receives, and he who seeks finds, and to him who knocks it will be* **open**.*"*
> *Luke 11:9-10*

6
Water

I was so excited that I could understand the Bible. I had to call my sister, Ann to let her know that I understood what I was reading from the Bible. The Holy Spirit gave me the understanding.

> *"The entrance of thy word giveth light;*
> *it giveth understanding to the simple."*
> *Psalm 119:130*

I must share what I experienced on the phone with my sister. It was very extraordinary. Her voice sounded like running water. Yes! It sounded just like running water. It was just incredible. All I could hear was the sound of running water, and we rejoiced together.

> *"Whoever believes in me,*
> *as the Scripture has said;*
> *Out of his heart will flow*
> *rivers of Living Water."*
> *John 7:38 ESV*

As I continue to talk about water, I will tell you about a dream that I had. I had a dream that I was in this beautiful river of crystal water that came up to my neck. This water was so clear and clean that it was like silver — very beautiful, very bright. I just floated in the water so peacefully. As I continued to float, a hand suddenly took me out of the water. I had nothing but peace being in the presence of the Lord! After what I had experienced, I woke up.

As I searched the scripture to see what the Bible said about what I had experienced, this is what I found: ***"Then the angel showed me the river of the Water of Life, bright as crystal, flowing from the Throne of God and of the Lamb." Revelations 22:1 ESV***

7
Bedroom Visitation

I had been reading a book on angels, and that night, I had a visitation. What I encountered was phenomenal! I had been praying for my sister who was in the hospital at the time. I saw her that night in my visitation, and I heard, "She is healed."

I sat up in the bed, and the room was filled with bright glittering light. The light was coming from a man right next to my bed, letting me know that my sister was healed. The peace, love, and joy all came from Him. His love is so deep, so pure, so loving. He was tall. He was wearing a long, white robe with sparkling gold coming from it. I could not see His face; just His presence.

> *"And his raiment became shining, exceeding white as snow; so as no fuller on Earth can white them." Mark 9:3*

As He got up from the bed to walk away, the train from His robe was so beautiful, and the peace of God filled the room. I got a call the next day that my sister was discharged from the hospital.

8

The Couch

One day, I had put my children down to take a nap. Everything in our home was so fresh and clean. My husband was at work. Since the children were taking a nap, I decided to lay down on the couch in the living room. When I did, I had no idea what was about to happen. It was phenomenal.

What I experienced took the fear of death away from me. I don't want to get ahead of myself. God is so good. I walked to the end of the couch and proceeded to lay down and put my head on the pillow. As I closed my eyes, the experienced I had was incredible.

My spirit came out of my body. God is my witness! I was out of my body looking at myself lying on the couch lifeless. I walked down the hall and checked on my children who were asleep. I turned around and walked back down the hall, back into the living room, and went to the end of the couch. I placed my feet where my physical feet were on the couch. Then I laid back and got back in my body and sat up.

While I was outside of my body, I was lifeless laying on the couch. I was DEAD! Yes! Dead! Once

The Couch

my spirit went back into my lifeless body on the couch, I became alive, and I said, "Oh my God!" I have no fear of death. I want everyone to know there is life after death.

> *"We are confident, yes well pleased rather to be absent from the body and to be present with the Lord." 2 Corinthians 5:8*

This encounter gave me a clear understanding about death. There is a separation from the physical body. This body is going back to the earth, and my soul to the presence of the Lord. I encourage anyone who wants a better understanding about death to read *Gone from My Sight: The Dying Experience,* by Barbara Karnes, RN.

9
The Floor

After cleaning up the kitchen, I proceeded to my bedroom. Just as I entered the doorway of my bedroom, I hit the floor, dropping to my knees with my face to the floor. I couldn't even lift my head because I was in the presence of the LORD.

He is HOLY!

All I could do was thank Him for loving me, saving me, and having mercy on me. The tears began to flow. I realized how messed up and unclean I was. When I say unclean, I was just that.

Even while I was in my mess, Jesus died for me. Oh, how I cried because I knew I wasn't worthy to be in his presence. In spite of my unworthiness, I experienced God's love. I thank Jesus for loving me.

I knew in that moment exactly why Jesus died on the cross for me and the world. When I was able to get up off the floor all I could do was weep. I was overwhelmed. God's love is truly unconditional. I am forever grateful.

"But God demonstrates His own love towards us, in that while we were still sinners Christ died for us." Romans 5:8

> "For he hath made him to be sin for us,
> Who knew no sin; that we might be made
> the Righteousness of God in him."
> 2 Corinthians 5:21

Reader, regardless of where you are, if you call on Him, He will answer. If you have never accepted Him, His arms are wide open waiting just for you. Come to Jesus, just as you are.

> "Everyone who calls on the name
> of the Lord will be Saved."
> Romans 10:13 NIV

> "Everyone who calls out to the Lord
> for help will be saved."
> Romans 10:13 GNT

> "For God so loved the world, that He gave his only begotten Son, that whosoever believeth in Him should not perish, but have everlasting life."
> John 3:16

> "This is how much God loved the World: He gave his Son, his one and only Son. And this is why: So that no one needs to be destroyed; by believing in Him,
> anyone can have a whole and lasting life."
> John 3:16 MSG

Hell is a real place. What I witnessed in hell was very shocking. It was terrifying. It is a dark place of torment. The smell is malodorous.

People in Hell were screaming, yelling, and crying out to God because they wanted to leave. Fire burns continuously in hell; it doesn't burn out. I heard people crying, "I'll forgive! I'm sorry! Please give me another chance God." I saw preachers in Hell yelling, "I will preach the truth!"

In Hell, I began to talk to some people. They knew my name, and this is what I heard, "Val, what are you doing here?"

Right after that, I heard someone say, "Evangelist Barr, what are you doing here?" Immediately, a hand reached down and pulled me out of Hell.

I was shaken so bad by what I had experienced. Now, I am telling my testimony. You don't want to go there. I pray that neither you nor your love ones go to that terrifying place.

The question is sometimes asked, *"If God is love, why does He send people to Hell?"*

Here is my answer to that: He doesn't send people there. People end up there because they have a free will to make their own choices. Luke 16:19-31 tells about the rich man and the beggar name Lazarus.

"There was a certain rich man who was clothed in purple and fine linen and fared sumptuously every day. But there was a certain beggar named Lazarus, full of sores, who was laid at his gate, desiring to be fed with the crumbs which fell from the rich man's table. Moreover, the dogs came and licked his sores. So it was that the beggar died, and was carried by the angels to Abraham's bosom.

The rich man also died and was buried. And being in torments in Hades, he lifted up his eyes and saw Abraham afar off and Lazarus in his bosom. Then he cried and said, Father Abraham, have mercy on me, and send Lazarus that he may dip the tip of his finger in water and cool my tongue; for I am tormented. And besides all this, between us and you there is a great gulf fixed, so that those who want to pass from here to you cannot, nor can those from there pass to us.

Then he said, I beg you therefore, father, that you will send him to my father's house, for I have five brothers, that he may testify to them, lest they also come to this place of torment. Abraham said to him, they have Moses and the prophets; let them hear them. And he said, No, father Abraham; but if one goes to them from the dead, they will repent. But he said to him, 'If they do not hear Moses and the prophets, neither will they be persuaded though one rise from the dead."

Reader, choose this day whom you will serve.

11

Heaven

Oh my! Heaven a grand place. The colors gold, yellow, purple, blue, white, and red are beyond any colors on this Earth. The flowers are so beautiful. The light is Jesus Himself. All the love, joy, and peace are from Him. They are beaming directly from Him. I didn't have a care in the world when I was there. All I wanted to do was stay with Jesus.

There is no love, peace, or joy like I experienced in heaven. I didn't want to come back, but I heard a voice that said, "It's not your time."

I was wrapped in a blanket of love. It was like liquid love that I can't even explain. All I know, is that everything I need is in Him. Heaven is real. Don't you want to go there?

"For our citizenship is in heaven, from which we also eagerly wait for the Savior, the Lord Jesus Christ."
Philippians 3:20 NKJV

"The Heavens declare the Glory of God; And the firmament shows His handiwork. Day unto day utters speech, And night unto night reveals Knowledge.
Psalm 19:1-2 NKJV

12

Joy

The joy that I encounter in Heaven is beyond being happy. This joy is so pure, so loving. It just goes down to your very soul. This joy is Jesus. He is joy. This joy is not man-made; it comes by way of the Holy Spirit. His joy will keep you when everything around is upside down.It's a joy that comes from the inside out. Jesus is that joy.

> *"And now come I to thee; and these things I speak in the world, that they might have my joy fulfilled in themselves."*
> *John 17:13*

13

Love

"But God demonstrates His own love toward us, in that while we were sinners, Christ died for us." Romans 5:8

God's love is unconditional. There is no love like God love. Real love is God. I don't know where you are at this moment. But before you believe the lie that nobody loves you, I want you to know that God loves you.

"Beloved, let us love one another, for love is of God; and everyone who loves is born of God and knows God. He who does not love does not know God, for God is love."
I John 4:7-8 NKJV

"For God so loved the world that He gave His only begotten Son, that whoever believeth in Him should not perish but have everlasting life."
John 3:16

"In this is love, not that we loved God, but that He loved us and sent His Son to be the propitiation for our sins. Beloved, if God so loved us, we also ought to love one another."
I John 4: 10-11

It is not the will of God that any perish. Will you pray this prayer?

Dear God, I confess with my mouth that I'm a sinner. Forgive me of my sins, and receive me as Your child. I repent of my sins, and I accept Jesus as my Lord and Savior of my life. I pray this, in the name of Jesus. Amen.

If you prayed this prayer, I encourage you to get into a Bible-based, Christ-centered, Holy Spirit-led Church. This is so you can continue to grow in your walk with the Lord. I pray this over everyone who reads *Spiritual Encounter: My Testimony*:

"The LORD bless you and keep you;
The LORD make His face shine upon you,
and be gracious to you; The LORD lift up
His countenance upon you, and give
you peace."
Numbers 6:24-26

God Bless everyone.

Thank you for your support!

P.O. Box 453
Powder Springs, Georgia 30127
www.entegritypublishing.com
info@entegritypublishing.com
770.727.6517

www.ingramcontent.com/pod-product-compliance
Lightning Source LLC
Chambersburg PA
CBHW042120100526
44587CB00025B/4132